Should I Go to College?

Dr. Chris Davis

DEDICATION

For the Western International University alumni, faculty, staff, and board members. The university maybe gone but our impact lives on in our graduates.

CONTENTS

1 INTRODUCTION

For me I don't think there was ever a time when I considered not going to college. My parents and my stepfather all had gone to college. I was good at school and enjoyed it. I never thought about whether to go or not, though where to go caused some consideration. Once I was there, I changed my mind more than once about what to study, but I never questioned going to college and then grad school.

Once I started working in higher education, though, I realized that college is not always the right choice for everyone, or at least, the timing must be right. Over the years I talked to many students who both graduated and those who dropped out.

The more time I spent in higher education, the more I began to see that college is not one singular experience. Different colleges offer different experiences for students. Students are not all fresh out of high school like I was. Most students today are over 25 years old often with full-time jobs and families. Even for students coming out of high school, increasingly they are the first in their families to go to college.

Only about 60% of students who start college finish within 6 years. That rate varies by institution, but I think part of the problem are students who start college when they shouldn't or without a clear understanding of the purpose of college. No one plans to fail.

In the last few years, there has been an explosion of books about why people should not go to college. Mostly written by people who did go to college, these writers claim that college is no longer worth the cost and that today anyone can learn anything worth learning online for free. Respectfully, I don't think that these writers have a full understanding of what college is and what it is not. I agree that for some people, learning online or through other non-college programs is the better path, but how do you know? A blanket statement that college is not good is not any better than a blanket statement that everyone should go to college.

College is expensive in terms of money but even more in terms of time and energy. My goal in writing this book is to help people make a more informed decision about whether they should go to college, and if so, how to decide where to go and what to study. I even talk about some of the alternatives to college.

The book is short, and I have compressed a great deal of advice based on over 20 years working in higher education as a professor, administrator, and student. If you find that you have specific questions, I have created a place for asking me anything about college and making the decision to go or not go. I answer these questions in a free weekly newsletter, so that others can learn from the questions. In my teaching career, it is rare when only one person has a question. It is more common that only one person thought to ask it.

To submit a question to me, use this link:

https://myheroicpath.com/ask-dr-chris-college-questions/

2 SHOULD I GO TO COLLEGE?

Why college?

Should you go to college?

Definitely maybe.

College is not for everyone, and it is not always the right time to go to college. Even if you know you should go to college and that the time is right, choosing a college and what to study are important additional questions. This book will help you answer these questions.

For over 20 years I have made my living from students who entered a university where I worked, so I do believe that attending classes and potentially earning a degree can be right for many people. I also have five degrees of my own and am considering going back for number six. I believe in higher education.

Having said that, if you do not know why you are in university, you should not be there. It is expensive and time consuming. If you don't have a purpose for why you are there, it will cost you. Maybe after a semester or several you will discover your passion and purpose, but there is a good chance that by then you will have taken courses that you do not need, and you will have increased your expenses without value.

I cannot in a book offer guidance that will fit everyone's life and circumstances. What I can do is ask some questions and give some advice that will hopefully help you make your own decisions. I do not guarantee that this book will make you healthy, wealthy, or wise. College like the rest of life is largely a result of what you put into it. My goal is to help you realize when you might not be able to get much out of college and make other plans. If you do decide to go to college, I will offer some additional advice about how to make the most of your experience.

What is your purpose?

The decision to go to college starts with knowing what your purpose is in going to college. Maybe you know your life purpose and maybe you have not figured that out yet. The question that matters is very specifically do you know why you think you should go to college.

If you do not have a clear answer to why you should go to college, then you should not go to college (at least not at this time.) You are free to read on, but you also might want to skip ahead to the last chapter on alternatives to college.

If you are not sure what purpose college would serve in your life, then read on to see if the examples and advice that follow help you make up your mind.

If you have your purpose, read on to validate that your purpose provides a good reason to go to college. I have known many people who had the best of intentions but when faced by the time and financial costs of college, their purpose faded.

Some people (but not many) have a life purpose that translates into their purpose in going to college. My college roommate knew in high school that he wanted to become a doctor, and he did. Today he works at a hospital that takes care of sick children. This was always his purpose, and it saw him through college, medical school, internship, residency, and fellowship. He spent a decade in learning what he needed to have the career he wanted.

I have another friend from high school that went to college, law school, passed the bar exam, and realized he did not really like law. He spent almost ten years going down a path that was not his true purpose. He went back to school, earned his doctorate, and now teaches at a university. Sometimes our purpose changes, and that is fine, but it is important that we be clear on

4

our purpose in going to college before we start and every step of the way. Only start if there is a purpose in doing so and leave as soon as that purpose is no longer relevant.

If you want to be a doctor or lawyer or another professional career, college is usually a requirement. I am not saying that you will always learn what you need to know in college, but a college degree is a requirement. The degree is the ticket that gets you invited to the dance.

A common purpose is the desire to start your own business. To be successful at starting a business, you probably don't need a college degree. You might be fine taking a few courses and then leaving. This drives universities crazy because it makes them look less successful, but Steve Jobs, Bill Gates, and Mark Zuckerberg all dropped out of college and most would consider each of them widely successful. In fact, I would argue that college is generally not very helpful if your goal is to start a business. Unlike employers, your customers probably won't care whether you have a college degree or not. The skills you need to run a business can be learned outside of college (see chapter 7 on alternatives to college).

For many young adults, the purpose for going to college is to satisfy family expectations. Parents who graduated from college typically expect their children to do so as well. Parents who did not go to college often want their children to have the experience and perceived opportunities that it brings. My advice is that starting college must be something that you do for yourself. If you are doing it because you are trying to please others, you run the risk of not being successful. College requires time, and unless you are motivated, it will be hard to make the time to be successful.

The psychologist and Holocaust survivor Viktor Frankl wrote that when the why is big enough the how will take care of itself. When your purpose in going to college is big enough, then you will find a way to pay tuition and the time to study. At the same time, if your purpose is not big enough, there won't be enough time and money, and you will almost certainly not finish what you start. You would be in good company, as many college students drop-out each year. My belief, though, is it is better to not start at all rather than fail.

A key consideration is where college would fit in your life. The traditional college model is a student who lives on campus and classes are the first priority. While some students put socializing first, they know that the reason they are in college is to be in college. Students who have the resources to have this type of college experience often have the purpose of college as an experience. They may also be looking to start a career in a professional field or to be positioned to land a first real job after graduation. It is a plus if you like learning, and you may be able to pick up some marketable skills along the way.

My college experience is an example of the traditional college experience. I started at the University of Michigan in September 1986, originally with the intent to go to law school after graduation. Then that fall my girlfriend dumped me, leading to a broken heart, and a desire to do something that I knew I would enjoy as a career…being a professor. I explored a couple of different majors starting with classical studies, then psychology, and finally ending up in sociology. My most significant learning took place outside of the classroom. I learned about customer service and leadership while working in the dorm cafeteria, and eventually I learned computer skills through a series of campus jobs.

When I started teaching in higher education in 1997, I taught a night class primarily for non-traditional students. At the age of 30, I was younger than most of my students. My students had full-time jobs and family responsibilities including spouses and children. For them, college was a pathway to advance in their career or start a new and better career. For traditional college students, college is their primary focus. For non-traditional students, college comes after work and family and often other interests.

Today, non-traditional students out number traditional students by a significant majority. While the traditional student population is decreasing, the non-traditional population is growing. Yet the stereotype remains of a college student as a young adult leaving home to attend college somewhere with a football team. When you have family and work responsibilities, college will not be the first priority. At best, it will be second priority and often third priority. For students with commitments to church or social organizations outside of college, college is a fourth priority. For these students, college for the experience of college is not usually the purpose, and if it was, they would be disappointed not having the time for the traditional student experience.

For non-traditional students, the purpose of college is work-related first. College can be used to start a new career path or to develop the qualifications to advance in an existing career. I will explore this topic more as it relates to how to choose a major in chapter 3. Even for some traditional aged college students with no other responsibilities, the purpose of college is career-related.

Unfortunately, many colleges continue to focus on the needs of traditional students. This topic will be important in the next chapter when I discuss how to choose where to go to college.

What is the purpose of college?

College creates value for students in two ways.

First, college is an experience. College offers four primary types of experiences:

Life experience: Traditionally, college has been a life experience for people age 18-22. For those with the resources to afford tuition and living expenses, college provides life changing experience. While the classes are important, what happens outside of class rather than in class is the most impactful aspect of the college experience. I learned leadership and management by working in the cafeteria more than in any classes I took.

Community: College creates an opportunity to be part of a community of people with shared interests. The community might be the college as a whole or it might be a subcommunity within the college. It might be a community around a certain major or it might be around a non-academic topic. Often college is the first time a student finds themselves in a tribe of people who share their passions.

Learning: You may enjoy learning and taking classes. Some people (myself included) like learning new things. This can be accomplished without going to college, but college provides a great environment for learning.

Achievement: College can be a personal milestone or goal. Or someone you care about wants you to be a college graduate. As I noted earlier, you need your own purpose independent of other people, but the expectations of others can be helpful. Every year a few people in their 60s and older graduate from college solely to achieve a personal goal.

The other value for college centers on career and work-related benefits to attending and graduating from college:

Professional Career. You may want a professional career that requires a college degree such as doctor, nurse, lawyer, engineer, accountant, etc.). There are surprisingly few professions that truly require a specific college degree, but many of those require a specific graduate degree.

Status: You may want an advantage in applying for jobs that do not really require a college degree but require or prefer one as a way of filtering applicants out. Many business and office positions fall into this category. Many management positions also fall into this category. The status of having a college degree can be used by employers to identify candidates for hire or promotion. A college degree is a simple way for employers to filter out candidates that do not have a degree.

Skill Development. You may want to learn specific skills for a job like graphic design or marketing or information technology. You can do these more cheaply outside of a college, but you can go to college for this reason. Sometimes, though, a college may lag what is used in the field.

People frequently focus on the career-related value that college creates. Colleges often focus on the experience and ignore or minimize the career aspects. Neither perspective is right or wrong. The important thing for you is to be aware of what your purposes are in going to college so that you can make the appropriate choices for you.

If at this point you do not see value in any of the purposes of college, then you should probably not be in college. College is expensive and time consuming. If you do not know why you are there, it will be hard to be motivated. You may take courses that don't help you later when you do know why you are in college.

Also, there are strong expectations for many graduating high school seniors to go to college. However, you do not need to attend college when you are

17 or 18. You can go when you have a good reason whatever your age. It is easier to go when you are younger and have fewer obligations but not required.

The chapters that follow will provide a more detailed analysis of each of these purposes for college including what alternatives there might be and how to decide what college to attend and what to study to maximize the value of college for you.

Key Questions

These three questions are key to knowing whether you should go to college:

- What is your purpose in going to college?
- Is college the best way to achieve your purpose?
- Is your purpose enough of a motivation to see you through to graduation?

Which of the seven purposes listed above apply to you right now? The great thing about college is that it will be there next month, next year, and ten years from now. If now is not the right time, you can wait until it is the right time. If you do not have a purpose for attending college right now, you should not be in college. Even if it was tuition free, college takes a lot of time. That time can almost certainly be better spent doing something else.

If you know your purpose, you need to evaluate whether college is your best option to achieve your goals. I will talk more about this when we look at the alternatives to college. In my experience, college is not the best option for some purposes. For example, if your purpose is to start a business, college is not a useful activity unless you want to have your own business as a doctor (or other professional field) since that requires a college degree.

Finally, you must ask yourself if your purpose is enough to see you through to graduation. Going to college full-time is the equivalent of a full-time job. Many people who start college because it is what their parents want struggle because it takes time. Sometimes people skip class or do not spend the required time on classes, which can lead to failing grades. It is much better to not attend college at all versus attending and failing.

3 WHERE SHOULD I GO TO COLLEGE?

Choosing where to go to college depends in large part on your reasons for going to college. Your campus experience will have an important influence on your experience of college. You also must consider your other requirements. If you have work or family obligations, you may be forced to consider options that are either local or online.

Campus Experience

The first step in determining where to go to college is determining your options for what type of campus experience you will have. You can live on or near campus. You can commute to campus traveling by car or public transportation to attend classes, visit the library, and participate in other activities. You can attend classes online and potentially never set foot on campus.

When you attend college and live on campus or near campus in student housing, and you work on campus or near campus, the campus is the center of your universe. Most of your interactions will be with other people associated with the campus. This is what we generally think of when we think of the traditional college experience. If your primary experience in attending college is the college life experience, your best option is a residential experience.

If you live with your parents or at least not with other students and commute to campus, then your college interactions will be fewer. The more hours that you work off campus, the fewer interactions you will have with others from the college. In fact, the more hours worked off campus, the less likely you are to stay enrolled to graduation. As a commuter student, you will still have the college experience, but it will not be the same as students who are on campus. This option can save money but commuting adds its own expense in time and money.

If you attend college online, your experience will primarily be the classroom experience. Online colleges often offer clubs or other online activities, but it is difficult to create the experiences of a traditional college. This option provides the most convenience and flexibility.

Some colleges offer low-residency programs. Typically, these are professional graduate programs designed for working students. Some classes and learning experiences are offered on campus potentially on weekends or in week-long residencies. Other classes are offered online. This hybrid approach offers most of the flexibility of online learning while still including some of the on-campus experience.

The first step in deciding where to college is to identify your options for where you can go to college. If you have family or work responsibilities that prevent you from re-locating to attend college, your options are limited to schools that are local, offer online courses and programs, or have low residency options where you only need to be on campus a limited amount of time.

If you have the flexibility to relocate, your options are much greater. Generally, being farther away from home increases expense for traveling back home and state schools offer discounts to residents. Tuition can be much greater attending a public college out-of-state. (In some states, though, the in-state tuition is high enough that leaving the state can be a better option.)

College as Life Experience

The traditional value of college has been the experience of attending college as a young adult making the transition from living with parents to becoming a productive member of society. College provides a unique opportunity to take classes, exploring a variety of academic and professional disciplines.

The real impact, though, occurs outside of the classroom. Campus jobs can become the foundations for post-college careers. In my case, my first management experience was in the cafeteria. My career in information technology began with a series of part-time jobs working with computers.

Except for joining military service, college provides a unique life experience that cannot be duplicated. The downside to the life experience of college is the expense. To maximize the impact, students should live on campus or at least near campus with other students. This adds room and board to the cost of tuition. Students need to be aware of the total cost of college attendance and not just the price of tuition.

While students can commute to campus and can participate in the campus experience, it is much more difficult. First, the time to commute to campus means less time for the college experience. Second, living at home can be a pull away from developing new relationships at college. If your purpose in attending college is the college experience and finding your community, living on or near campus is by far the best option. The good news is that this also opens you to the most options about where to go to college.

If your goal is learning or the achievement of being a college graduate, you have more options. You can attend college on campus or online. Commuting will be less of an issue if your goal is the degree more than the traditional college experience.

College for Career Preparation

If your purpose is to use college to develop career opportunities, how you attend college will depend on your career goals. The ABA only accredits law schools that are face-to-face, so online law school is of limited value if you want to take the Bar exam and practice law. Some areas of study clearly are best done in-person, like surgical technology or welding or most types of engineering. Any study that requires special equipment or physical manipulation of tools or supplies is best done when the professor can provide immediate feedback on student performance and coach on proper procedures.

Some career programs are offered at a limited number of schools. When I was first a dean, aviation was one of my programs. Very few colleges have aviation programs. We had students who came from many states away for this program. If you have a career in mind, your research might identify a limited number of options for study.

Personal Feasibility and Preference

A major consideration in where to go to college is what is feasible for you. If you have work, family, or other responsibilities, then your only options might be attending something local or online. While this makes it a challenge to have the traditional college experience, but if your goal is to obtain a college degree, then this is not an issue. Online education has grown largely to serve the needs of non-traditional students who could not quit their jobs and move their family so they could go to college. Community colleges and career colleges also tailor their offerings to students who need to study at night or in accelerated programs that provide the quickest path to graduation.

Even if you can move to go to college, you may not want to. I went to a good high school in a small city in Michigan. Almost everyone in my high school who went to college went to a school in the state of Michigan. Meanwhile, I had friends in the suburbs of Chicago where almost everyone went out-of-state for college. The difference was tradition and expectations. You must find what is right for you. I applied for five college, and three were out-of-state. One of those turned me down, and in the end, I picked the University of Michigan because it was much less expensive than the other options. Even though I was only 2 hours from home, I went home rarely, and I stayed in Ann Arbor during the summer to work and study.

The key question is whether you can and desire to move for college and if so, how far. While the colleges I applied to were private schools more expensive than Michigan, sometimes the less expensive option is farther from home. Travel might be an additional expense, but if you are only planning to come home for Thanksgiving, the holidays, and maybe summer, that does not need to be a huge cost. The real question is whether you and your family will be okay if you only come home a few times a year. This is a very personal issue with no right or wrong answer except for the answer that works for you.

If you know you need to stay local or attend online, this narrows your search for colleges. If you can travel, then you have a wider set of colleges to select from. Generally, you will want to narrow your search down to an area just to make your research more feasible.

Most people visit colleges in the summer. This is a convenient time for high school students, but it is not the best time to visit campus. First, students are not on campus, which makes it harder to get a sense of the community. Second, weather in the summer is very different than in the winter. Maine is beautiful in the summer, but unless you really like snow, it is less so in winter. In college, you will spend a great deal of time outside walking between classes and other buildings.

Another set of factors to consider is the community for the college. Colleges can be in urban areas where the campus is a seamless part of the city. The Loop area of Chicago is home to multiple colleges and even has student housing though the campus buildings look like the office towers that are their neighbors. Colleges can also be in suburban areas of cities. Northwestern University's main campus is just north of Chicago, where it has a traditional college campus, yet the city is easily accessible. Other colleges are in small towns and rural areas. Miami University of Ohio has a lovely campus in Oxford, Ohio with no local expressways and not much to the town beyond the university.

Each of these settings offers advantages. Urban colleges mean being part of an urban environment with the cultural and social opportunities that go with a big city. A small-town campus means a greater focus on campus life and activities on campus. What type of space that makes sense for you depends on you, and it is worth visiting to get a sense of what you like and feels comfortable.

I know a daughter of a colleague from the suburbs of Chicago who started college in New York City. After a year, she transferred to a college in downtown Chicago. One of her frustrations in New York was that most of her classmates were close enough to home they would take a train home for the weekend. She only lasted one term in Chicago. The program she was in was mainly online, so she did not have much opportunity to find a community of interest with others in her major. Her third stop was a university in rural Illinois where she has found her place. Her biases and perceptions had ruled-out this school early in her decision-making process. She also started college thinking she was there for professional career preparation, when her real purpose was the life experience.

Types of Colleges

The official Carnegie classification of colleges includes seven categories of colleges in its most basic categories. When including sub-categories, that number increases to over thirty. In my opinion, most of the differences matter mainly to people who work in higher education. I am not going to try to recreate a classification system, but I think it is important to review the broad categories of institutions as it relates to the student experience.

Research Universities
These are the most famous type of institution often with a national reputation. Most states have at least one flagship university that is a research university. These are usually public universities, but they can be non-profit. The focus is on faculty research, and undergraduate courses are often taught by graduate students. Often, they have a hospital system attached to the university. More often they have significant athletic programs. These are very large organizations and very complex.

Regional Public Universities
In most states, there is another tier of public universities that lack the prestige of the flagship school and other major research universities. Typically, they will have graduate programs, but more courses will be taught be faculty and usually without the large lecture halls. Many of these schools began as teacher colleges and over the last fifty plus years they have diversified to include much more than preparing teachers. (If you see the term "normal college," this is the old term for a teacher's college.) Most have residence halls, but they serve primarily students from the local region.

Liberal Arts Colleges
These are usually but not always private, non-profit colleges. Many were started by religious movements. In the 19th century, every Protestant faith felt the need for their own colleges, especially as seminaries to prepare church leaders. Over the century since, many have lost their religious background while some are still very connected to their denomination. They tend to be residential with students living on campus with most

courses small and taught by full-time faculty. Increasingly they are adding professional graduate programs, but this has not been their focus. They usually have athletic programs, but not ones with a high profile.

Career Colleges

Career colleges have historically been for-profit schools but not always. For-profit colleges are businesses that provide educational services. They may be dedicated to a specific profession like cosmetology or they might have a broader set of programs in healthcare, business, and technical fields. These were some of the first colleges to offer online programs, though in the last several years many other, more traditional colleges have been adding online programs. Programs at career colleges tend to be focused on a specific career pathway. Career college campuses tend to be commuter campuses, but some do have residence halls.

Community Colleges

Community colleges are public colleges based in a local area. They usually have two-year programs that prepare students to transfer to a four-year school along with two-year career programs. In some states, they have started to offer four-year degrees. Community colleges usually are commuter colleges, but some have residence halls.

The different types of college do not mean much when it comes to quality, but they do provide some framework for understanding the differences in student experience between different institutions.

Prestige

A key aspect of a college degree is the prestige that goes with being a college graduate. That prestige reflects the reputation of the school where the degree is earned. Reputation is how the university is perceived by others.

Reputation and prestige come from many sources. College rankings are one source. The rankings are not based on any measure of quality of outcomes from the school. Instead other measures are used to rank schools, many of them subjective. Peer reviews, how other colleges perceive a college, are part of their ranking process. Another factor is how many people apply to the school and how many are accepted. The faculty are also a factor.

Faculty who are famous either in their field or beyond academia boost their institution. Research generated especially funded research is also a factor. Having programs that are well known in their fields also can help. Athletic programs (especially football and basketball) also build university brands. How pretty the campus is can contribute to reputation. Famous alumni also help. The alumni network can help people land jobs in some fields, and the size of the alumni network is important.

While it can be beneficial to graduate from a more prestigious university, prestige itself is not an indication of how good the college is. There are roughly 4,000 colleges and universities in the United States. Most people probably have heard of maybe 40 of those nationally. In regions and local areas, colleges may have a local reputation, which can be valuable when you are living and working in that area. Do not put too much weight on the prestige of the university.

Major and Choice of College

In the next chapter we discuss how to select a major. If you have a specific major in mind, then you will obviously need to find a school with this major. When I was a campus dean, one of my programs was aviation. Very few colleges have aviation programs, so this limits the options for students who want to go to college to become a pilot.

Researching Options

The first step in researching options is to determine what type of institutions that you are looking for based on your purpose.

If your priority is the college experience, then you want to focus on schools that have residence halls. Even if you will not live on campus, having students on campus is what creates opportunities for activities and clubs. You will next need to determine what you can afford and your own preferences. How important is it to be near home or far away from home? Farther away is usually more expensive because of additional travel expenses, but this can also be offset by lower costs for tuition and/or housing.

If you want to be within a certain distance from home whether that is 30 minutes, 1 hour, 4 hours, or 8 hours, you have a geography to look at schools. You only need to search out the schools within that range. If location is not a factor or even if it is, you will want to consider whether you want urban, suburban, or rural/small town. This further reduces the list. If distance is not a concern, you may have preference for a certain region of the country.

If you need to be able to commute to campus, then your options will be limited to what is near you and online options, unless you do not want to do online. Since so many colleges offer online programs now, there are many options for online study.

Key Questions

Once you have limited your search to a limited set of schools, you need to do the research that will help you determine which are your best options.

For each option you can identify, you should ask each of the following questions:

- What is the reputation? (Positive national, positive regional, neutral, negative)
- Does it have the major?
- Career Services for field? Placement rates?
- What are options if that major does not work out?
- Policies on transfer and alternative credit?
- Campus experience?
- Term length?
- Accreditation?
- Are classes online?
- What is the cost?

Reputation is not the sole factor, but it is worth considering how the college is perceived.

If you know what major you want to study, having that major is important. It is also useful to know if they provide career services for that major and what the placement rates are for graduates. Also, you should know what your options are if that major does not work out. Some programs only admit a few students, and if you do not get in, what are your other options?

Policies on transfer credit and alternative credit can change the total cost of your degree. It is best to shop different schools to see who gives you the best deal.

The campus experience is important, even if your primary purpose is career development. Do you feel comfortable on campus? Do you connect with other students?

The term length is important both for how long you will be in school and your experience. Many career schools use accelerated courses, so each class might be 4-weeks, 8-weeks long, or 10-weeks long versus the traditional semester of 15-weeks. Shorter classes can meet a quicker path to graduation, but that also means more intense studies with more study time each week.

Accreditation includes two areas. First, the school itself must be accredited either regionally or nationally for students to receive financial aid. Credits from regionally accredited schools tend to transfer more frequently than those from nationally accredited schools, but that is the primary difference from a student perspective. Second, some programs need program accreditation to allow students to receive licensure. This varies by program and state, but it is something to consider. You may have issues if you receive a degree in one state and want to practice in another state. One of my friends discovered that her degree in massage therapy from Michigan lacked the required number of hours to be licensed in Kentucky. This is something to consider, if it pertains to your major and career.

Online courses are important if you want to study online, but they can also be an advantage even if you are on campus. A good question to ask is what you will ever need to come to campus to do. Schools may offer online courses but still require exams on campus.

Cost we will consider in a later chapter, and cost can be different than the published cost. It is something you will want to have some idea on as you decide about where you want to go to school.

At this stage, you should have a list of schools that would meet your needs. Cost may remove some schools from the list. If you are applying to selective schools, you might not be able to get in everywhere. After all of that, trust your instincts about what option feels like it best meets your purpose in going to college in the first place.

4 WHAT SHOULD I STUDY IN COLLEGE?

Purpose and major

Selecting a major and degree depends on what your purpose is in attending college. If your primary purpose is college as an experience, then it does not matter what you study. If your primary purpose is using college to launch a career, it matters what your major is for some professional careers, but not at all outside of those few career paths.

College as experience

It does not really matter what you study if you are looking for the experience of attending college. I encourage people to select something they enjoy. College requires many hours of study and classes, and the experience will be better if you are studying things that you enjoy.

You should study what you are interested in learning. If you are interested in a variety of things, then take a variety of courses. Most college degrees offer flexibility in what you can take as electives or to meet distribution requirements, but this is something to pay attention to. Also, learning for the sake of learning can usually be achieved without enrolling in a college degree program, which we will explore in a later chapter.

The type of community that you want to be part of is also a factor in deciding on your major. If you are an artist, chances are you will want to hang out with other artists. The best way to do that is to take art classes, and while you can take art classes as part of any major, you will take more if art is your major. Substitute music or theater or computer programming or any other topic for art. At the same time, if you don't know what your community is, college is a great place for exploring and discovering your place and people. You do not need to know that when you start, and in traditional schools, you don't pick a major until your second year at the earliest to give you time to explore.

If your goal in college is the achievement of graduation, you will want to pick the major that is something you will enjoy and offers the shortest path to graduation. In the next chapter, I will discuss transfer and other forms of credit that can decrease your time to graduation. Different majors even at the same college can go faster.

College for career preparation

Many people outside of higher education feel that the purpose of college education is career preparation. Even through that narrow lens, there are variations in how a college degree translates into employment.

The most direct connection is when a specific major is required for a professional career. Many professional careers that require college require a specific degree and/or major. This includes careers as diverse as barber/cosmetologist, truck driver, accountant, schoolteacher, engineer, lawyer, and doctor. The level of degree varies. Many career programs only require a certificate, a diploma, or an associate degree. Other careers like law and medicine require graduate degrees. Teachers, accountants, and engineers can usually get by with a bachelor's degree, though a graduate degree in these fields can be helpful.

If your goal is to earn a college degree for the status of being a college graduate, the major is not relevant. Again, I recommend majoring in something that you enjoy. You might also look at what major will give you the quickest path to graduation. The end goal here is having a degree and what the degree is in is irrelevant.

A frequent criticism of the liberal arts and liberal arts majors is that they are not aligned to a career path. My undergraduate major was sociology. I enjoyed sociology, learned valuable things about how to conduct research, but my career in information technology was based on a series of on-campus jobs that developed my IT skills.

College is generally not the best place to learn marketable skills for employment unless it is part of a degree aligned to specific career. Accounting majors learn some useful concepts and processes as accountants. In general, though, technology means that most skills are out-of-date within two years. In a four-year degree, only skills learned in the last year will be relevant for the job. College was not designed for this type of learning.

College can be effective for developing soft skills like communication and problem-solving, but these general skills are not career specific. They apply to all majors and are part of the value of a college degree in general for employment opportunities.

The key for developing marketable skills in college is to find jobs or volunteer opportunities that allow you to develop and practice real world skills to create value. In job interviews, it will be these experiences that will demonstrate your potential value to an employer and not what you covered in class.

If your purpose in attending college is to develop your career opportunities, you should start by identifying what career you are interested in and researching what type of education and training is required. Working backwards, you can identify whether college is a requirement, and if so, whether a specific degree or major is required.

As part of your research, you should also look at whether a career requires that you graduate from an accredited program. Some professions require state licensure, and these requirements vary by state. For a lawyer to take the BAR exam in every state except for California, she/he must have attended an American Bar Association (ABA) accredited law school. While most law schools are ABA accredited, not all are. In contrast, there are three accreditors for business programs, but I am not aware of any state that requires accountants to have studied in an accredited business program to sit for the CPA exam. Each state has similar requirements on what a student has studied, and generally it takes more than four years to meet these requirements. Most business majors do not have professional licensure for people working in the field, so program accreditation is not a requirement for professionals. To become a teacher in most states, you must graduate from a teacher prep program licensed by the state, which may mean that the program is accredited in some states.

In general, if you know you want to work in a specific state, you should look at the requirements in that state. I know someone who graduate with a degree in massage therapy, but when she moved to a new state, she discovered her program did not have enough hours of practice, so she could not get licensed. These rules vary widely from state to state and profession to profession, and often colleges are only familiar with the requirements in the state they operate. Upfront research can save you a great deal of pain later.

At this stage in your decision-making process you should know whether you need a specific major and degree or if any major will be acceptable. If possible, it is best to put off deciding on a major as long as possible. You will know more tomorrow than you do today and waiting will help you make a better choice. Unfortunately, for some careers, you need to know what your degree will be before you start.

Selecting a major

At traditional colleges, you are not typically expected to select a major before your junior year. The thinking is that your first two years you are exploring different subjects and taking your general education courses that are required for all majors. In this setting, there are few risks that you will take a course that you do not need for graduation or that you will miss a class that you will need. The major is generally the focus on the last two years, and even then, you will have some flexibility to take courses outside of your major. This is what a liberal arts education is all about. The "liberal" means taking a variety of classes in your education. It has nothing to do with politics.

The exception to this generality is when you are pursuing a specific career path that requires you to be admitted to a particular college from the start. Engineering is a great example of this. Typically, students apply to engineering versus liberal arts, and the course requirements will be somewhat different. Even in this case, though, you will not select an engineering major until the second year. Business and education schools often start in the junior year, so at the same time you would be declaring a major, you might be applying to one of these programs. Nursing can vary. You might start in nursing from day one, or you might apply to nursing school later in your studies.

Some professional fields like law and medicine do not have undergraduate majors. These professions are studied in graduate school. While some colleges may offer "pre-law" or "pre-med" as a major, the reality is that any major can work, though for medicine you need to take specific science and math courses.

It is possible to do a double major where you take the required courses from two majors. Some colleges also have minors where you take fewer classes than a full major and the minor is listed on your transcripts. Usually these options do not add much to your qualifications. The exception would be in secondary education where your major and minor will restrict what subjects you can teach in high school.

In addition to traditional colleges, other colleges focus on career preparation. Often in these schools, you must declare a major from the time that you start, and many of your classes may not be used by all majors. If you change your major, you may find yourself with courses that do not apply to your degree.

Community colleges offer both types of programs. Transfer programs are general and designed to allow someone to transfer to a four-year college to earn a bachelor's degree. Career programs are specific to a career path, and while they may also transfer to some four-year programs, the curriculum tends to be very focused on a specific field of study.

Accounting provides a great example of how these differences play out. At a traditional college, you would spend the first two years without a major, taking general education courses and courses required to apply to the business college such as calculus and economics. In your second year, you would then apply to the business school, and if accepted, could select accounting as a major. At a career school, you would select accounting as a major when you apply to the school. You would probably begin taking accounting classes in your first year. At a community college, you could either do a transfer program and apply to a business college, or you could pursue an associate degree in accounting. At the end of the2-year associate degree, you could leave school to pursue employment in an entry level accounting position as a bookkeeper or accounting clerk. You could also apply to business school. You could also apply to a four-year accounting degree at a career school. While you can be an accountant without being a Certified Public Accountant (CPA), CPAs command higher salaries and prestige. The requirements to be a CPA vary by state, but they all include additional study after the four-year bachelor's degree. Accounting is the most complicated major and career path in the different pathways that are available, but the example shows the different approaches to declaring a major and how that varies by the type of college.

Key Questions

As you consider your major, there are three critical questions to answer:

- What is your purpose in going to college?
- How does a major align with your purpose?
- When do you need to decide on a major?

Your purpose in going to college should dictate your choice of major. In general, your major only matters if your purpose includes using college as a pathway to a career that requires a specific major. At career colleges, typically you will have to articulate a major and career pathway at the time you begin studies if not sooner. At traditional schools, the major is less important regarding a career pathway. My recommendation in both cases is that you should major in something you enjoy. College is hard. It requires a great deal of time. You should get some pleasure out of the process. Studying something you are interested in will make it easier to stay in school through graduation and often will lead to better grades. If there is nothing that you like studying, then you should be reconsidering the choice to be in college at all.

You should put off making a final decision on a major as long as possible. The more classes you take and the more you learn about different majors, the greater the chance you will want to switch majors. You will always want to be aware of what classes apply to many majors and which are specific to a major. If you take courses that you later do not need, it will increase both the financial expense and time to graduation.

5 HOW DO I PAY FOR COLLEGE?

College can be expensive both in money and time. There are some ways to reduce the financial costs, and virtually anyone can afford to go to college. Cost, though, is a key factor in deciding where to go to college as prices vary a great deal.

In addition to the cost of tuition and fees, college includes an opportunity cost. The hours spent in class and studying could be spent working. Attending college full-time is like working a full-time job. Typically, this means if you are working more than a few hours a week, you will need to go to college part-time. This further means it will take you that much longer to earn a degree. Going half-time means not graduating for 8-10 years versus 4-5 years. Students who do work more hours and try to study as well are at greater risk of dropping-out. It can be done, but it is not easy.

Almost everyone can find a way to pay for college using student loans and grants. The risk is graduating with substantial loans that must be repaid that make it difficult to buy a house or pay other bills.

A long time ago, I had the choice between a very nice private liberal arts college and a state university that was considerably less. I did the math, and the difference would help pay for grad school. I opted for the state university. I don't regret that decision, and I was fortunate that my parents had the resources to pay for my undergraduate studies. College was also cheaper back then.

My rule of thumb is that you should not borrow more for college than you would for a car. If you can afford that Tesla, go for it. If you can afford a used Honda Civic, go for that.

Here are things to consider:

1. Do you hope to pursue a career that will involve grad school? Not only will that be more money for school, but it matters more where you goes to grad school than it does undergrad.

2. Unless you go into a career like accounting or engineering where you start earning a decent salary right away, the loans will be a challenge upon graduation. It will be harder to choose a job that is important to you for reasons other than money or to start a business.

Private schools offer on average a 50% tuition discount. You can shop around to see what college will give her a better deal. It is possible that a college with a high published cost might be less than a public university.

Some neighboring states may have lower tuition than schools in your own state. It is important to shop around.

Community college for a year or two also reduces the total cost of degree significantly.

Federal student loans for dependent students are limited. If you are claimed on your parent's taxes, you will not have as many federal loans as someone who is independent. As a dependent student, you can either ask your parents to take out parental loans or co-sign loans with you. If you do this, your parents should take out a life insurance policy on you with enough coverage to pay off the loans. If something happens to you, then they won't be stuck with your loans.

Financial Aid

Some fortunate students have the money (or their family has the money) to pay cash for school, including not just tuition and fees, but room and board and textbooks.

For everyone else, there is financial aid. Financial aid is a big and complicated topic and largely beyond the scope of this book, but it is important to address a few basic ideas.

First, financial aid can come from multiple sources. This section is very specific to the context of the United States and may or may not resemble the experience in other countries.

The federal government provides a significant amount of financial aid. This includes grants that do not have to be paid back (think of these as government scholarships) and student loans. How much aid you can receive and of what type depends on your financial status (how much money you make and how much money you have in the bank and other factors). It matters whether you are a dependent of your parents or if you are independent. An independent student can take out more federal loans than a dependent student. At the time of this writing, any student can receive federal student loans (with a few exceptions) regardless of credit. Even if you could not qualify for a credit card or a car loan, the government will loan you money to go to school. The federal government also provides financial aid for veterans and government employees including active duty military.

Another source of financial aid are state governments. These programs vary by state. Often they are "need based," which means they go to students with less personal and financial resources to attend college. States also directly fund public colleges and universities, which means lower tuition rates for state residents. Displaced workers may also have access to state grants for college.

Colleges and universities also have institutional aid which are scholarships that the school pays for out of their own budgets. These can be need-based or merit-based where they are awarded to students with high grades and test scores or who participate in athletics. Some scholarships are funded by alumni or other friends of the school who have established a fund for a particular purpose such as students who graduated from a specific high school. Some institutional aid will be automatically granted to students, and other aid you will need to apply for. One of the purposes of the financial aid office is to help identify potential sources of aid.

While some people set-up scholarships with specific schools, other scholarships can be used at any school. I met someone who received a scholarship for red heads. I need to find this one, because five of my ten children are red heads. Schools may have information on some of these, but many scholarships you will need to track down on your own.

Employers often offer tuition assistance as a job benefit. Even companies with part-time employees such as Walmart, McDonalds, Starbucks, and Manpower have college programs. I was personally involved in creating a program with Manpower where their temporary employees could earn an undergraduate degree with no out-of-pocket expense. Companies are using these programs not just to reward existing employees. They are often designed to attract and retain employees. It might be worthwhile to look for employment with a company that offers educational benefits.

In addition to federal loans, there are also private loans for college expenses. These loans are like car and home loans and borrowers must meet eligibility requirements. Unlike other loans, these loans can rarely be wiped out even in bankruptcy. They are an option, but an option that should be exercised with caution.

In summary, there are many ways to get money to pay for college. You will need to talk to the financial aid office at your school about options, and you may need to do some additional research on scholarships from other sources and through employers.

Loan Limits

My strong recommendation is that you should plan on finishing your undergraduate degree with zero debt. First, many students whether they graduate or not discover large monthly payments after graduation. At the same time, when you are just starting out in a career, starting salaries can be low. Student loans may limit your options of where you can work, whether you can start a business, or if you can buy a house.

Student loans are deceptive. You do not usually have to pay while you are in school, so they are easy to ignore until you are no longer in school. This can lead to a big change from not having any payments to have a very large payment.

The other risk with student loans is that you can take out more than just the tuition, fees, books, and direct costs for school. In the short-term, the additional loan money seems like a windfall. You can pay rent, buy nice things for yourself and your family, but when you are no longer in school that extra money will go away and will need to be paid back. This means you will take a double hit on your cash flow.

Also, if you attend graduate school, you may need loans then. Taking out undergraduate student loans will limit your flexibility later in that regard as well.

The best approach is not to use loans at all. If you do use loans, you should request only enough money to pay for tuition, fees, and books. The key to achieving this is to maximize on other sources of financial aid and minimize the expense of college in the first place.

Transfer credit and prior learning assessment

One way to reduce the costs of college is to earn credit before starting college.

For high school students, there are Advanced Placement (AP) courses that are taken in high school and then an exam is taken that can be used for college credit. It is possible to earn credit for a semester or more this way.

In many states, high school students can also take duel enrollment classes. These are college classes taught in the high school for credit for both high school and college. Some states cover the costs, though in others there are tuition charges. I have heard of students who graduated college before graduating from high school. This varies by state and locality, but it is an option that can reduce the time and money spent on college.

For those of us who are out of high school, there are still options for advanced credit. Rather than Advanced Placement exams, there are CLEP and DANTES exams that anyone can take for a small fee. Many colleges will accept scores from these exams for college credit.

If you have military experience, many colleges will accept military training for credit for courses. Even if you are not in the military, many colleges offer prior learning assessment (PLA) that will give you credit for certifications, workplace training, and even your work experience. These policies and programs vary. Some schools do not charge while others do, though it is almost always less than tuition.

Credits that you earned at one college can also be transferred to a new school. The policies depend on the new school, and unfortunately not all colleges are transfer friendly. Transfer credit is one of the most frustrating aspects of higher education. The institution receiving the credit is the one that decides what if any credits are accepted and what they are used for. Schools may give a preliminary review and then reverse it later.

The key strategy with these forms of credit is to shop around to different colleges. Look into policies and ask for a preliminary review of your credits. A difference of one course being counted or not can be worth a $1000 or more.

Community College

The first year of college is the hardest. Most people who drop-out do so in the first year. I believe that the main issue is that students start college without a clear purpose, and quickly exit when the experience of college fails to provide value.

One way to mitigate this risk is to start at a community college. This will be much less expensive than a four-year college. If you cannot be successful at the community college, you would not be successful at a four-year college.

Community college tuition is usually the most affordable college tuition. Starting at the community college, and then transferring to another college or university will reduce the total cost of a bachelor's degree by almost half. When you add room and board of living on campus versus living at home and commuting, the savings can be even greater.

Community college courses are usually smaller and taught by professors in contrast to most public universities where courses can be large lectures and courses taught by teaching assistants.

If your purpose is college for a career, community colleges typically have a variety of career programs than can be completed within a year or two. In many places the community college may have specialty programs aligned to local employer needs. These programs maybe the only feeder into certain careers and employers.

Often community colleges have been viewed as last options. This is an unfair perspective. In many cases, community college are the best choice for a student. This is especially true for career programs that are often not available at four-year institutions.

Hacks for Majors

One way to "hack" your college education to save money and time is to look at alternative career paths that require less education to achieve similar outcomes.

Nursing vs Doctor

To become a medical doctor requires a bachelor's degree plus three years of medical school and a minimum of three years in residency. That is a minimum of ten years of education. In contract, to become a nurse's assistant requires a CENA that is covered in 1-2 courses. A licensed practical nurse requires 1-2 years of study, a registered nurse a two-year degree. A Bachelor of Science in nursing can be earned while working. Now a nurse will not make what a doctor makes, but a nurse will start working sooner and with less debt. More importantly, a nurse can go to grad school and within a year or two add qualifications such as nurse anesthesiologist or nurse practitioner. These credentials command very attractive salaries without the time or expense of medical school or the expense of malpractice insurance. A Doctor of Nursing is almost as prestigious as an MD with less time and money. We have a shortage of MSNs, which we need in higher ed to teach other nurses.

Also, if you discover you hate sick people, you can do something else without investing years of school. You can also argue emotionally than nurses are more engaged with patient care than doctors. With uncertainty about changes in medical care and government regulation, being a doctor might not be a great option in the future. Even now, nurses are taking on a larger role in medicine.

Plus, you can always apply to medical school after graduating as a nurse. Nursing offers more flexibility and opportunity than just going to medical school.

In addition to nursing, there are a variety of healthcare professions that lead to fulfilling work with education that ranges from a one-year certificate to a master's degree. When we think about healthcare we tend to think about doctors and nurses and not respiratory therapists or x-ray technicians.

Counseling vs Psychology

Many people have a desire to help others. The traditional path is to go medical school to become a psychiatrist or earn a doctorate in psychology to become a therapist. Both options are long and expensive.

The alternative is to pursue a master's in counseling. These programs are typically two-three years after a bachelor's degree. There are online options available. At the end of the program, you will be able to counsel and work with clients. Therapists make more money, but they will also be paying more for their education.

Other Careers

If you have your heart and mind set on a specific career, it is worthwhile to research what alternative careers exist that lead to similar work with less educational requirements. You can always go back to school to earn more degrees, and the quicker you get out of school and to work, the quicker you are fulfilling your purpose.

Key Questions

When considering how to pay for college, think about these questions:

- How much can I afford to spend out-of-pocket?
- How much financial can I expect to receive?
- What will be the cost of tuition, fees, books, and materials?
- What can my employer provide in tuition assistance?
- How can I reduce the expense of college?

Your goal should be to not use any student loans. With that in mind, you need to know how much you can afford to pay for school. It maybe that you have no savings or discretionary income, which does not mean you cannot or should not go to school, it just means that you need to be even more strategic in your approach.

The amount of financial aid will vary in part by school. Do not assume that the published rate is what you will pay. Private, non-profit schools may offer scholarships. Also, schools may keep tuition low and have significant fees. Make sure you know the full price of attending. Shop around for the best deal. Even online, prices can vary a great deal. My wife attended a public college out-of-state that had low tuition for their online programs. Even when studying on campus, schools out of state might be cheaper than state schools in state.

Make sure you find out what your employer will provide for tuition assistance. Also check with your parents' and spouse's employers as they may have family benefits. You might want to look at changing jobs or getting a second job for the educational benefits. You might also consider the National Guard or Reserves.

Finally, you will want to consider your options for reducing the expense. What courses can you earn prior learning credit? (Remember to check with schools you are looking at in advance as what they accept is different.) Should you go to a community college for a year or two? Is there another program that will lead to a similar career?

Cost should almost never be a barrier to going to college. However, it can have a significant influence on where you should go. More expensive is not always better.

6 SHOULD I GO TO GRADUATE SCHOOL?

The question of attending graduate school follows the same decision-making process as the decision to get an undergraduate degree.

What is the purpose of graduate school?

Graduate school tends to focus on career preparation in a specific career path. Several careers including law, medicine, and counseling require a graduate degree. In the liberal arts, graduate degrees have primarily served as the entry point for becoming a professor.

Students in graduate school have usually found their identity and their calling. The graduate school experience focuses on exploring a field in more detail. At the doctoral level and in some master's programs, research and the writing of a thesis plays a central role.

Graduate students fall into two primary categories. Students in professional programs spend 2-3 years on campus before graduation. Students in doctoral programs spend 6-10 years on campus before graduation. For the students learning a profession, the focus is on course work. For the doctoral students, there are courses, but more time will be spent in a combination of teaching and research. Large research universities rely on a pool of graduate assistants to work on research and teach undergraduate courses.

Traditionally graduate school like undergraduate education was campus-based. Graduate students generally moved to or near campus and school was the primary occupation. This started to change with programs such as executive MBAs that were designed to meet the needs of working adults who could not quit their day job to go to grad school. These programs offered intensive courses on weekends as an alternative. Over the last 20 years, though, online learning has created more opportunities for students to study while keeping their job and not having to relocate to campus.

Some programs, especially doctoral programs, that require extensive physical laboratories do not translate to an online environment. Other programs such as the traditional MBA on more prestigious campuses persist in part because large companies and consulting firms continue to recruit from campuses. Other programs, such as law, are limited to campus-based delivery due to accreditation requirements. Research universities still offer on-campus doctoral programs in part because they need the labor of doctoral students to support teaching and research.

For someone looking for the traditional college experience, graduate school can offer this experience. However, most graduate students are looking for career advancement over the college experience.

What are the prerequisites for graduate school?

All graduate programs require that students have a bachelor's degree. Beyond that basic requirement, there is a great deal of variation. For some universities, the degree must be from a regionally accredited college or university.

Some programs are competitive. In these cases, you will often need to take an entrance exam. The GRE is used by many programs, but law school has the LSAT, business the GMAT, and medical school the MCAT. In competitive programs, you will often need letters of recommendations frequently from former professors. You will likely have to write essays as well. In competitive admissions, the status of where you did your undergraduate studies will matter. In some professional fields, whether you earned an undergraduate degree from an accredited program in that field may make a difference.

In addition, some programs may require specific undergraduate courses. If these were not part of your undergraduate studies, you may need to take them prior to applying to admission or in some cases after you have been admitted to the program. In many cases, federal financial aid cannot be used for these courses because the courses are not part of a degree program.

Many master's degree programs do not have special requirements and start multiple times a year. Others may start only once or twice a year, and in these cases, paying attention to deadlines is very important.

How do I become a professor?

One of the common reasons for going to grad school is the desire to become a professor. I have written a book on this topic already, and if you are interested, you should check out "How to Become a Professor?" on Amazon. I will repeat some of the core advice from that book here.

The first general rule is that you should have a degree higher than the students you are teaching, so to teach undergraduates you should have at least a master's degree and to teach graduate students, a doctorate. In some areas, there is no doctorate degree, so whatever the terminal (highest level) degree is appropriate.

The second general rule is that you need 18 graduate credits in the area you are teaching. For example, if you want to teach accounting, you need a master's degree plus 18 graduate credits in accounting. The master's could be in anything, but usually it will be in accounting. If you have an MBA, you may or may not qualify depending on how many accounting classes you had at the graduate level, and not all colleges and universities will count work experience. Sometimes a professional designation might be enough. In accounting, a CPA even without a master's degree should be credentialed to teach undergraduate accounting.

A frequent issue that I have seen are people who pursue a graduate degree in education. The logic is that since they want to teach, they should get a degree in education. Unfortunately, higher education and K12 education are not the same systems and have different requirements. Very few master's or even doctorates in education have 18 graduate credits in anything other than education. Most colleges of education primarily teach people who want to be K12 teachers, so they hire professors with that kind of experience.

If you want to become a professor, you should pursue a graduate degree in the subject you want to teach. Ideally you also have professional experience in this field. In most cases you will need a doctorate. Even if you have all these things, the academic job market is very competitive, and it is difficult to find a part-time job let alone a full-time one.

Should I get a Master of Business Administration (MBA)?

The MBA is one of the most popular graduate degrees. Since it is a professional degree in business, on the surface it appears to be a path to advance or start a career in business. Since most undergraduates do not have an education in business, the MBA appears to be the next step for anyone not interested in healthcare or technology careers.

In the beginning the MBA was designed for exactly this reason. Students would graduate with their undergraduate degree, work in business for five years, and then if they could afford it and did not have family obligations, they could go back to school for a residential MBA program that was an additional two years of study. At graduation, consulting firms, financial services companies, and other major companies would be waiting to hire the graduates, at least at the high-status schools. At these schools, MBA tuition was (and is expensive). The two-year program was generally more than the cost of a four-year undergraduate program.

In time, the high-status business schools started offering an executive MBA option for individuals who could not leave their jobs for two years. This option was even more expensive, but usually employers paid the tuition to develop high potential employees. The executive MBA was offered on weekends and in short sessions so that students could continue to work full-time.

Less prestigious universities also started offering MBA programs for non-traditional students. With the development of online education, these programs expanded even further. They offered the flexibility of allowing students to work and study but at a much lower tuition than executive MBA programs.

These three different MBA programs served very different audiences. The traditional MBA was for students who could study on campus for two years with the intention of landing a high-paying job after graduation with a large company. The executive MBA served the needs of executives who had companies willing to pay tuition. The other programs served everyone else.

Over the last few years, some of the traditional MBA programs have closed. This reflects a decline in the number of traditional students overall. Instead these institutions are focusing on both existing executive MBA programs and offering their own online MBA programs to non-traditional learners.

The decision to pursue an MBA should be based on your purpose in earning the degree. If your goal is to work in consulting or finance, and you can both be accepted into a traditional program and afford it, you should be good to go. If you have an employer willing to pay for executive education program, then this can be a great option. The networking with other students alone is valuable, especially when you need a job in the future.

If you are working in a business and your ability to advance or change companies would be enhanced by having an MBA, the degree makes sense. If you are looking to move into managing people, an MBA will provide you with a broad understanding of business and management that will support your career.

An MBA alone without business experience, though, will be of less value. A more specialized degree might be better at creating new career opportunities.

Is a master's degree the new bachelor's degree?

For employers having a bachelor's degree is often the requirement for some positions or is used as a differentiator between two candidates. Since many more people have bachelor's degrees today compared to the past, a question is whether having a master's degree is the new minimum requirement for careers. The professional term for this is "degree inflation." The answer is that it depends. In some fields, like occupational therapy, positions required a bachelor's degree in occupational therapy. Today the master's in occupational therapy is the minimum, and some advocate for a doctoral degree as the standard. In that type of case, then yes, the master's is the new bachelors. More generally, though, this is not the case.

The value of a bachelor's degree is only partially in the content of what is studied. The value comes from the ability to meet the requirements of an undergraduate degree. Even in professional fields, most employers recognize the need for on the job training for new graduates. The programs that do not expect to have to train new graduates are those like nursing where clinical experiences and internships during the degree provide the same function as on the job training.

The master's degree lacks this type of general value. The master's degree focuses on a single subject, and the value depends on how important that subject views graduate study. In some cases, earning a master's degree in a subject where you are already working may increase your opportunities for advancement. This depends on the company and industry.

Can a master's degree be used to change careers?

Some master's degrees are designed to help you change careers. The Master of Arts in Teaching, for example, is designed to take someone with an undergraduate degree and prepare them to be a K12 teacher. Other master's degrees in technical fields and healthcare can be an entry into a career in that field. The Master of Arts in Counseling is the entry level degree to become a counselor.

In other cases, the master's degree is only of value to people with work experience in that field. Usually this is clear from the admission's requirements to a program, but it is worth verifying that the degree you are considering will offer the career benefits you hope it will before you invest time and money.

When using a master's degree to change careers, it is important to investigate what career services are provided by the university for graduates from the program. Having the degree is of little value if you cannot find jobs to apply for or have difficulty in getting interviews.

Often a career change can be accomplished without an additional degree. Other educational opportunities might be enough to develop skills. Your existing employer may be willing to let you work on projects with other departments or create a path for you to transition to a new area within the company.

Rarely but sometimes you need to go back for a second bachelor's degree. I have a friend who was an elementary school teacher who went back to school to become a nurse. That required a second undergraduate degree.

Key Questions

If you are considering graduate school, you have four questions to consider:

- What purpose would a graduate degree serve for you?
- Would an alternative to a master's degree achieve the same result for less time and money?
- What and where to study?
- How will you find the time for graduate study?

A key aspect of undergraduate education is the experience outside of the classroom. Graduate education is more centered on professional education. You should be able to validate that the promotion or career change you hope to make will be enabled by a master's degree and what specific degree will achieve that goal.

Related to this, a variety of alternatives to traditional education exist. These include online programs, certificates, and bootcamps that provide skills training that can reduce the need of a graduate degree. While many jobs require an undergraduate degree, few require a graduate degree.

Once you know that a master's degree is needed for your goal, you can research what major and school. The major should align to your purpose. If you are going to attend a traditional, face-to-face program you will be limited to locations within a reasonable commute. If you can relocate to attend a residential program, you have more options. Online education offers more options but can be limited in available programs.

An online search for specific programs will provide a list of options that can be reviewed for the curriculum and price. For some programs, program accreditation is a key consideration. This is mostly true for programs that require professional licensure. These requirements vary by state, and it is important to review the requirements for the state where the student intends to work after graduation.

Graduate study can be on-campus but is increasingly online. In either case, it takes time. Before starting grad school, think about where the time for school will come from. Traditional undergraduates have school as their first priority. Adults who go to graduate school have work, families, and friends.

7 HOW CAN I INCREASE MY CHANCES FOR SUCCESS IN COLLEGE?

Why do students fail?

After almost 25 years working in higher education, the primary reason I have seen for students who are successful comes down to time. Ability including learning disabilities can be overcome, but a student who does not or cannot invest enough time in class will fail.

Tennis legend Jimmy Connors said that, "I never lost a tennis match, I just ran out of time." The same is true for college students. They run out of time.

A good rule of thumb is that for every semester hour of credit a student should expect to spend 45 hours of work. That includes in-class time as well as homework and study. It does not include travel time to campus. In a traditional 15-week semester, that is only 3 hours a week. That is not so bad. Most classes are 3-4 credits, so it is 9-12 hours per week for one class. Most people do not have an extra 9-12 hours a week with nothing to do. Full-time study is a minimum of 12 credits, so that requires 36 hours per week. That is almost equivalent to a full-time job.

Many colleges and universities offer accelerated courses where the number of weeks is reduced. This also means the time required per week is doubled. One class offered in an 8-weeks is going to require about 18 hours a week.

Traditional students that live on campus and have school as their primary focus should be able to carve out time for school. Those who don't usually do not stay in school. Most college students today are non-traditional students. They are usually working. They often have families to take care of. They have interests in friends, church, and other activities. Something must give to allow them to be successful in school. That something must go for the years it will take to earn a degree.

Some students will give up. They may doubt themselves and their abilities. They may sabotage their success by avoiding doing schoolwork or attending class. Sometimes family and friends will pressure students to stop going to school. While many families do celebrate the first person to get a college degree, others are afraid that the college graduate will leave them behind and stop being the person they were. They may also resent the time spent on school versus family or social activities. Traditional college students living on campus around others focused on education have some buffer against these pressures.

Students can also waste time. As a professor, I have seen students try to solve problems on their own when they are stuck rather than reaching out for help. A professor or a tutor might be able to help the student see what they are missing very quickly rather than spending hours on something that is unproductive.

If students thought about how they were going to budget for the time that classes take like they think about how to pay tuition, more students would be successful. Very few people have a time hole in their lives. For most, college requires stopping something you are doing now.

How can I prepare for college?

In addition to being clear on your purpose and how you will make the time to study, a little preparation can increase your success in college.

Most schools have some sort of placement test that identifies your current ability in math, reading, and writing. If you do poorly on these exams, you may need to take additional courses to get your skills up in these areas.

Most schools downplay the importance of these exams because most prospective students do not like the idea of an exam. Ask if there is a practice exam that you can take and do a little study on these topics before the exam. It is all material you have seen before, but most of us do not think about things like fractions or punctuation daily.

Do I really need to take math?

Math classes are required in virtually every undergraduate degree. They are one of the most feared courses as well. In talking to students, I find them most of them have been traumatized by previous attempts to learn math. This stress makes it emotionally difficult to learn in college.

A primary source of the problem is that math is really a foreign language, but it is not usually taught that way. For example, if I ask you what is "½ / ½" ? You need to know that the one over two is one-half and the slash means divide. Now if I tell you that .5 / .5 means the same thing, you might question how this can be since they do not look like the same thing. However, if I tell you that we half a pie left and we are going to share it evenly, you can probably figure out that we are each getting a quarter of a pie. Math people skip the pie and just use code to talk about the same idea. You must learn to understand the code to be able to do math. When we start talking about cosigns and tangents, it is even harder to understand what is going on because the code becomes even more removed from the real world. Engineers make great math teachers because engineers are used to applying math codes to real world problems.

If math is a struggle for you, as it is most students, be patient with yourself. Learn it like you would a foreign language. Use tutors and other students to help you grasp it.

Some majors require a solid understanding of math. If that does not sound like you, then you should carefully consider other majors. Science, engineering, and technology fields are the most common ones that use math, but chefs use fractions more than anyone. Nurses also need to be good in math so they do not give someone the wrong dosage of a drug.

What if I don't like to write?

If you don't like to write, you need to get over it. While many careers do not require heavy duty math skills, almost all careers require people to communicate effectively whether it is in presentations, emails, or reports. In college, papers and essays are a standard way of assessing what you know. Writing skills are important.

You should take your composition class as early as you can. While most academic writing is different than the type of writing people do in the real world, the foundation of being able to express yourself and your ideas clearly and effectively is a universal skill you can develop with practice.

The most important concept in academic writing is the five-paragraph essay. Paragraph one is an introduction that catches the reader's attention, tells them what you are going to say, and end with a thesis statement which is the point you will prove in the rest of the essay. Paragraphs two, three, and four each start with a sentence that summarizes the point you will make in that paragraph. The other sentences in the paragraph provide more detail. Together those first three sentences should summarize your argument. Finally, the conclusion (paragraph five) summarizes how you have proven the point you made in your thesis statement.

For example, if your thesis is that you like turtles, you might start your introduction with a description of turtles or some other device to start your story. Paragraphs two, three, and four will each be a reason why you like turtles: because they are easy to catch because they are slow, because they are cuddly, and because they eat salads. Finally, in your conclusion you summarize why you like turtles.

That basic structure is how you craft an essay in virtually every college class. If you need to write a paper, you add more paragraphs. You might even structure the paper as a series of essays where each essay builds on the previous one.

The other key to academic writing is the use of citations.

Plagiarism is one of the quickest ways to end your college studies. Plagiarism is using someone else's ideas without proper documentation that these are not your ideas and where they came from. The most obvious example is using words or pictures that someone else has created. Anytime you quote someone, you need to use quotation marks and cite the source of the quote. Most of the time you will not (should not) use direct quotations.

Instead you put into your own words what someone else wrote. In this case, you don't need quotation marks, but you still need to cite the source.

One way to think about this is that you are making an argument. Is it stronger to say that something is your opinion, or is it better to say that an expert on the topic said this? The expert has more credibility, so it is in your interest to give credit to the expert and how she/he supports your argument.

When you do not cite someone else's ideas, you are committing plagiarism. Not only does this make your argument weaker, it also means that you are stealing someone else's ideas, even when you do not us their exact words. Even if you do this unintentionally, you can fail an assignment or worse.

Different schools use different formats for how you cite your sources, and you should ask your professor or teaching assistant if there is a required style. If you are new to academic writing, it can be a good step to check your writing for plagiarism before you submit it. I have worked with 1000s of faculty, and many are not very forgiving when it comes to plagiarism.

Every so often someone famous will be caught having plagiarized a speech or document, leading to the end of their career. Learning how to properly cite sources and avoiding plagiarism is a valuable skill.

Why does failure matter?

Starting college but not graduating is not the end of the world. Having some credits has value, and it is always an option to start again later. Having said that, there are consequences to starting and failing.

First, there is a psychological barrier about starting and then failing. It can feel like a defeat, and it can be harder to come back if you believe that you will fail again.

Second, if you took out student loans, those loans must be paid back whether you graduate or not. It will be much better to graduate then to be paying on loans when you did not finish.

Third, if you stop attending class or stop submitting assignments in the middle of a class, you will likely fail those classes. That will make it harder to start again at the same school. It can also make it so that you cannot get federal financial aid in the future. You can also be financially responsible for financial aid that you received and did not use because you stopped attending classes. You should never stop attending classes in the middle of an academic term unless there are extenuating circumstances, and you should always talk to an academic advisor and a financial aid advisor about your circumstances.

What is your purpose again?

When a student chooses to do something other than schoolwork, it reflects a choice about values. Helping a child with their homework reflects a priority on being a parent. Helping a friend move reflects a priority of service to others. Going out with friends to see a movie reflects a value of social connection. Few people go take courses because they like to read textbooks and write papers. The key to making good choices is to remember why you are in college beyond the classes. What do you hope to do with that degree? When you think about your purpose, it will help you prioritize your time.

If you follow my advice from chapter one, you start college with a strong purpose for being there. College is a marathon, though, and it is easy to forget that bigger purpose. Unfortunately, not all classes and not all assignments will align with your purpose. Sometimes you must jump through hoops to earn the degree. Remember your purpose to keep up your motivation to get it done.

Sometimes your purpose will change. There is nothing wrong with that. It is your life to live. Every day we learn more, and some days we learn that the path we were on is not the right one anymore. Your purpose in going to college might not be relevant anymore.

Do you need to leave school?

If you find that the right decision is to leave school even just for a break, there are several issues you will want to avoid.

Whenever possible, finish classes you have already started. You cannot get all your tuition money back or your time. If you can finish out the class, you will have those credits for the future.

If you need to stop in the middle of a class, do not simply stop attending. Contact the college and formally withdraw, but before you do, make sure you review what the impact will be on your financial aid. Often students are not aware of what is known as "return to lender." The federal government has loaned you money or potentially provided grants for you to go school. If you leave without attending enough of the classes that were paid for, the school must return the money to the government. The school will then charge you for this money. If you do not pay it, you will not be able to take classes there or even order a copy of your transcript. Do not assume that you are okay because no one told you it would be a problem. Make sure you talk to someone in financial aid.

Even if you have finished classes, you should contact the university before withdrawing and make sure your schedule is updated. I talked to someone once who was billed for a class that was after he left and had a difficult time getting it cleared. You also want to verify any financial aid impacts. Different schools follow different calendars and policies, so every school is different. Ask questions and get it in writing. If they won't send you something in writing, email the school with a summary of the conversation and ask them to confirm your understanding. Unfortunately, you may need these types of records later.

Key Questions

Before starting a degree program at any level, it is important to review how prepared you are for success. Specifically, consider these items:

- How much time can you commit to school?
- What support can you expect from family, friends, and at work?
- If you don't have the skills in reading, writing, and math required for college, are you prepared to develop these skills?
- If you are commuting, do you have reliable transportation options?
- Do you have a computer and Internet access to do homework?

School requires time and there are no short cuts. Usually the time required is every week that classes are in session. Rarely in my years as a professor, have I seen students work ahead. To be successful in school requires commitment of time.

It also requires commitment from other people in your life. This is true at home, but also with friends who may not understand why you do not have as much time for them. Work can also be a challenge when unexpected work assignments interfere with meeting deadlines for school.

Most students in college today are adults who have not been in the classroom for years. It is okay to not be current with academic writing and math, but you need to be ready to develop those skills. That might require getting assistance outside of class from professors or tutors. Keep in mind that academic skills are generally not the same skills used in everyday life. The key is to do what it takes to be successful, and after the first term, classes will be easier.

I was visiting a rural campus one time and a student told me that one night both of his cars were broken down, so he drove his tractor to get to class. That is dedication. Missing a class requires a student to work even harder to cover what was missed. Having plans and back-up plans for how to get to class is important, and if you miss class try to find out what you missed before the next class session.

Online education removes the need to get to class, but it does require a computer and Internet access. Even traditional classes have homework that will require a computer and Internet access. While it is possible to use computer labs and libraries, it is much better to have access to your own computer.

8 WHAT ARE THE ALTERNATIVES TO GOING TO COLLEGE?

With the large amount of information online, a common question is why go to college when everything to know is online. This is a misconception of what college provides in terms of both learning and credentials, but there are opportunities to develop skills outside of the college classroom.

What do teachers do and why can't I just teach myself?

When the printing press was invented, many expected the end of classroom teaching since everyone could learn from a book. Clearly this did not happen. Likewise, the Internet does not mean the end to learning from a teacher.

Teachers, including college professors, do many things. First, they curate and select content. They decide what information students should learn and what does not need to be covered. A student can have access to massive amounts of information online, but it can be overwhelming to find what is useful to know. Teachers also sequence the content in a way that supports learning.

Teachers also provide assignments that allow students to apply and demonstrate what they are learning. Teachers then provide feedback on that work to help students correct errors and improve. Teachers can also answer student questions and provide encouragement to increase student motivation. A learning studying on their own does not have that type of support.

When a student finishes a college class, the course and final grade is recorded on a transcript. An employer can see the transcript as demonstration of what a student has learned. A student that is self-taught does not have this type of validation.

Other Learning Experiences

College professors are not the only places to find teachers. A wide variety of online courses exist that include teachers. In addition, seminars, workshops, and bootcamps offer face-to-face learning experiences. Many of these offer certificates of completion to document the class.

Online, many colleges offer MOOCs (massively open online courses). While some of these can be taken for free, certificates and feedback on assignments usually require payment of a fee. Some companies also offer courses related to their software. In addition, many independent teachers offer online courses.

These online learning experiences can sometimes be used for college credit. Some universities allow MOOC students to use their MOOC courses in undergraduate or graduate programs. You will want to verify this with the college or university where you intend to enroll, but it is a way to reduce the expense of college. Other colleges will award credit for experiential learning or prior learning assessment. This varies by school, but it is something worth asking about to save money and time.

Bootcamps have been a feature of IT education for decades though they have expanded in the last several years. Typically, these are face-to-face, intensive experiences to develop certain technical skills like web design. A bootcamp lasts only a few months and usually provide some assistance in finding employment at the end of the program. They are usually not cheap, but shorter and cheaper than a college degree.

Most of the students in MOOCs and bootcamps are college graduates who use these programs to develop marketable skills after graduation. Some employers will still prefer someone with a college degree. These options may work best as an alternative to a graduate degree for someone with a bachelor's degree.

Careers that do not require college

Many good careers do not require college. For a variety of reasons, technical and career education has decreased in most high schools. This has contributed to less awareness of the need for people working in skilled trades such as plumbers, electricians, carpenters, and other professions. These are professions that require skills but not a college degree.

Starting a business

Many people have a goal of starting a business. College is generally not well suited to preparing you to start a business. The exception are professional services like law and medicine that require a college degree to practice.

There are many paths to starting a business. One option is to buy a franchise which usually includes training from the company you buy the franchise from. Another option is to buy an existing business. You can also create a business from scratch.

To start or manage your business, you need to know how to either do (or hire someone else to do) a variety of business functions including accounting, marketing, product design, sales, customer service, and so on. College business courses tend to focus on how business is conducted in mid-large sized companies where departments handle each of these functions. These courses are not well-suited for being a one-person operation.

There are many classes online, books, and other resources for entrepreneurs. Some of them are very good and others are not. At the end, though, you must put it into practice.

I recommend that someone start with an affiliate marketing business. Affiliate marketing means that you sell someone else's product and receive a commission. Amazon, for example, has an affiliate program where you can link to any product on their site and receive a commission on any sales that come from your web site. This means you must do the marketing and build an audience of people who purchase from your site. You do not need to invest in creating a product. The key here is that if you cannot sell established products, it is unlikely that you can sell something that you would create on your own. Affiliate marketing allows you to develop and test your marketing skills, and if you can do that, then you can move on to creating your own products to sell.

Many businesses can be and should be started as a side gig to a full-time job so that you are not relying on the business to pay the rent. Once you grow your business to the point you are earning more on the side, then it is time to think about quitting your job.

Going to college to learn to start a business slows you down from this process. It is better to use your time starting a business, learning by doing, and getting to your purpose than it is to go to school so that someday you can start a business. For most businesses, the customer will never ask you about what degrees you have earned. They will only care about the value that you can create for them.

Key Questions

A degree program is not always the best option if you need to learn new skills or credentials. While it is unlikely that these alternatives will totally replace higher education anytime soon, it is worth considering what alternatives you have to achieve your goals. Consider these questions:

- What alternatives are there beyond a degree?
- Can you learn on your own or do you need a structured learning experience?
- How are you going to pay for an alternative?
- Is the alternative compatible with your life?
- How will you stay motivated in a course or program?
- At the end of the learning, how can you demonstrate your expertise to employers?

In some cases, there are no alternatives. Professional programs often require a specific degree. For example, to become a licensed counselor, you need to complete a master's in counseling. In other cases, especially in technology and business, there are other options for learning. Sometimes colleges and universities offer certificates that are shorter than a degree program that might meet your needs. When you know why you need additional education, the next step is to do some research to see if there are other options.

Sometimes you can teach yourself using books and online resources. Sometimes, though, you need someone to teach you. Teachers provide a variety of services beyond just presenting content. You need to think about whether this is a topic that you can teach yourself.

One of the benefits of higher education is access to federal financial aid. Most alternatives to higher education do not have access to federal loans and grants. This may require you to pay the costs for the learning out of your own pocket. Some courses are free or low-cost, but others are very expensive. Even when an alternative exists, it might be more affordable to pursue a degree.

Some alternatives such as bootcamps require daily attendance for a period of months. This type of intensive learning is faster than taking a course one night a week, but it also requires that you be able to commit to the schedule. Alternatives might not be compatible with work or other commitments. Other programs are online and might be more flexible, but you will want to include this in your research.

Staying motivated is a challenge in any learning situation. In higher education, professors and advisors are there to help you stay on track and follow a schedule. Learning on your own or in a self-paced course requires motivation to keep learning and progressing. The completion rate for MOOCs is very small. Without someone holding you to a deadline, it is easy to put off learning, thus delaying achievement of your goals.

Some alternatives have certificates of completion or other ways to demonstrate what you have learned. In some programs you may have projects that you can use to demonstrate what you have learned. Employers are used to college transcripts and degrees, so it can be a challenge to demonstrate what you have learned outside of higher education. This is something to consider before choosing an alternative path.

9 WHERE DO I GO FROM HERE?

A successful business must ask what products to develop that customers will want to buy. If you think of yourself as a business, you need to think about what products (skills, expertise, experience) that you need to develop to be successful. Like a company, you have limited resources to invest including time and money. College is an investment, and you need to make sure your investment will lead to the results that will create value for you.

You should not start college without a clear purpose and a plan to finish. If you buy a car and do not like it, you can sell it to someone else. Let's say you buy a car for $10,000 and sell it after one year. Even if you only receive $5,000, that is better than nothing. If you go to college for a year and decide to leave after paying $10,000 in tuition, you will not be able to get any of your money back. College is too expensive to view as an experiment. The advice in this book will hopefully help you avoid costly experiments.

This book is short. I am not a writer who says the same thing in different ways many times. I have also tried to provide advice that is concrete and can be used to make better decisions.

I have avoided including links to web sites and other resources because these links can change. Instead, I have created a web page with links to additional resources that I will keep updated:

https://myheroicpath.com/should-i-go-to-college-resources/

One of the challenges of writing a book like this is that everyone has a unique story. Educational and career opportunities vary significantly by where you live. Each person has her or his individual background with school and work that will influence their future options.

If you want to ask me an individual question, you can do so at this link:

https://myheroicpath.com/ask-dr-chris-college-questions/

If you don't have any questions, you can still subscribe to my weekly college advice newsletter to see what questions others have.

My goal is to provide objective advice about whether college is right for you, and how to decide where to go and what to study. If I can help you with these questions, please let me know.

ABOUT THE AUTHOR

Dr. Chris Davis started his teaching and research career in 1992 and has worked with universities and other organizations around the world. His teaching experience includes courses in business, information systems, and psychology. He writes about learning and education.